FAITH'S LITTLE INSTRUCTION BOOK
FOR MOMS

Harrison House
Tulsa, Oklahoma

Unless otherwise indicated, all Scripture quotations are taken from the King James Version of the Bible.

Scripture quotations marked NIV are taken from THE HOLY BIBLE, NEW INTERNATIONAL VERSION®, NIV® Copyright © 1973, 1978, 1984, 2011 by Biblica, Inc.™ Used by permission. All rights reserved worldwide.

Scripture quotations marked NLT are taken from the Holy Bible, New Living Translation, copyright © 1996, 2004, 2007 by Tyndale House Foundation. Used by permission of Tyndale House Publishers, Inc., Carol Stream, Illinois 60188. All rights reserved.

Scripture quotations marked NKJV are taken from the New King James Version®. Copyright © 1982 by Thomas Nelson, Inc. Used by permission. All rights reserved.

Scripture quotations marked MSG are taken from The Message. Copyright © 1993, 1994, 1995, 1996, 2000, 2001, 2002. Used by permission of NavPress Publishing Group.

Scripture quotations marked AMP are taken from the Amplified® Bible, Copyright © 1954, 1958, 1962, 1964, 1965, 1987 by The Lockman Foundation Used by permission." (www.Lockman.org)

Scripture quotations marked NCV are taken from the New Century Version®. Copyright © 2005 by Thomas Nelson, Inc. Used by permission. All rights reserved.

Scripture quotations marked NASB are taken from the NEW AMERICAN STANDARD BIBLE®, Copyright © 1960,1962,1963,1968,1971,1972,1973,197 5,1977,1995 by The Lockman Foundation. Used by permission.

Scripture quotations marked WE are taken from THE JESUS BOOK - The Bible in Worldwide English. Copyright SOON Educational Publications, Derby DE65 6BN, UK. Used by permission.

Scripture quotations marked Phillips are taken from The New Testament in Modern English, 1962 edition, published by HarperCollins.

Scripture quotations marked TLB are taken from The Living Bible © 1971. Used by permission of Tyndale House Publishers, Inc., Wheaton, Illinois 60189. All rights reserved.

15 14 13   5 4 3 2 1
Faith's Little Instruction Book for Moms
ISBN: 978-1-60683-686-6
Copyright © 1996, 2013 by Harrison House, LLC.
Tulsa, OK 74145

INTRODUCTION

Faith's Little Instruction Book for Moms is a powerful collection of quotations by dynamic Spirit-filled women of our day. This book provides insights of wisdom for training children in areas such as building relationships, faith, learning responsibility, intercession and following the leading of the Holy Spirit.

Faith's Little Instruction Book for Moms is a treasury of truth and applicable knowledge that will renew your mind with the light of God's Word.

God has given parents tremendous responsibilities. Along with these responsibilities, however, God has given tremendous power to carry out what He requires. The power that God gives to parents is in His Word.

Marilyn Hickey

Now all glory to God, who is able, through his mighty power at work within us, to accomplish infinitely more than we might ask or think.

Ephesians 3:20 NLT

Our children and grandchildren are covered in our covenant with God. Everything God gives to me, He'll give to them. All protection that I have, He passes on to my family.

Gloria Copeland

❧

Know therefore that the Lord your God is God; he is the faithful God, keeping his covenant of love to a thousand generations of those who love him and keep his commandments.

Deuteronomy 7:9 NIV

God commands us to be overcomers. The first place we must overcome (the Devil) is in our domains. We don't have authority over our neighbors. But we have authority at home.
Billye Brim

Behold, I give unto you power to tread on serpents

and scorpions, and over all the power of the enemy:

and nothing shall by any means hurt you.

Luke 10:19

Teach (your children) properly in the Word and live the Word before them. They will be a pleasure to you.
Pat Harrison

Provoke not your children to wrath: but bring them

up in the nurture and admonition of the Lord.

Ephesians 6:4

God is concerned about the peace of your children. He wants to bless you and your family, but you must choose the blessing. You must choose life for yourself and for your children. And life comes through God's Word.

Marilyn Hickey

All your children shall be taught by the Lord, and

great shall be the peace of your children.

Isaiah 54:13 NKJV

When we teach our children properly in the Word and live the Word before them, we are fulfilled with beautiful children.

Pat Harrison

As arrows are in the hand of a mighty man, so are children of the youth. Happy is the man that hath his quiver full of them: they shall not be ashamed, but they shall speak with the enemies in the gate.

Psalm 127:4-5

Children don't understand the unseen forces that are coming against them. So it's your responsibility to stand against those forces on their behalf.

Gloria Copeland

Therefore, put on every piece of God's armor so you will be able to resist the enemy in the time of evil. Then after the battle you will be standing firm.

Ephesians 6:13 NLT

When you rule God's way, your children will not only respect and obey, but they will desire to please you.

Sharon Daugherty

For the Lord corrects those he loves, just as a father corrects a child in whom he delights.

Proverbs 3:12 NLT

when you feel your emotions welling up within you, try quoting the Word of God rather than spouting your emotional outrage.

Carol McLeod

Do not let any unwholesome talk come out of your mouths, but only what is helpful for building others up according to their needs, that it may benefit those who listen. And do not grieve the Holy Spirit of God, with whom you were sealed for the day of redemption.

Ephesians 4:29-30 NIV

It is important for parents to live the Christian life before their children.

Oretha Hagin

Do all things without murmuring and disputings:
that ye may be blameless and harmless, the sons of
God, without rebuke, in the midst of a crooked and
perverse nation, among whom ye shine as
lights in the world.

Philippians 2:14-15

Once you get things straight between you and your husband, you'll have a lot more power where your children are concerned.

Gloria Copeland

Husbands, in the same way be considerate as you live with your wives, and treat them with respect as the weaker partner and as heirs with you of the gracious gift of life, so that nothing will hinder your prayers.

I Peter 3:7 NIV

God made you to flourish and to inexaustibly thrive. He did not make you to die on the vine of life. He spiritually designed you for emotional and spiritual abundance in every season of your life.

Carol McLeod

The righteous will flourish like a palm tree, they will grow like a cedar of Lebanon; planted in the house of the Lord, they will flourish in the courts of our God. They will still bear fruit in old age, they will stay fresh and green, proclaiming, "The Lord is upright; He is my Rock, and there is no wickedness in Him.

Psalm 92:12-15 NIV

Parents should not only teach their children, but they should set a godly example in the home.

Oretha Hagin

Be ye followers of me, even as I also am of Christ.

I Corinthians 11:1

No matter what you say to your children, they are going to follow your example – whether good or bad.
Pat Harrison

Speak and act as those who are going to be judged by the law that gives freedom.

James 2:12 NIV

While your children are growing up, they might forget some of the sermons you've preached, or act like they're not interested in the things of God. However, they will never forget your example.

Gloria Copeland

Train up a child in the way he should go: and when he is old, he will not depart from it.

Proverbs 22:6

Children will usually become what their parents are.

Oretha Hagin

Imitate God, therefore, in everything you do, because you are his dear children.

Ephesians 5:1 NLT

Your example will go a lot further than your words.

Gloria Copeland

Those things, which ye have both learned, and received, and heard, and seen in me, do: and the God of peace shall be with you.

Philippians 4:9

From the time you hold your child in your arms, you begin to whisper in its ear, "God is your Creator and your Father. Jesus is the Lord of our home." That child's spirit is alive unto God from the time he is born into this earth.

Pat Harrison

❦

As you know not what is the way of the wind, or how the spirit comes to the bones in the womb of a pregnant woman, even so you know not the work of God, Who does all.

Ecclesiastes 11:5 AMP

If you begin to confess what God's Word says about your home life and your family members, you will begin to see that nothing is impossible because you will come under the authority of the Word.

Marilyn Hickey

This is what the Scripture says: "The word is near you; it is in your mouth and in your heart." That is the teaching of faith that we are telling.

Romans 10:8 NCV

There is one important thing about applying the Word. You must look into it, see who it says you are and – despite all natural appearances to the contrary – you must believe it.

Lynne Hammond

But whoever looks intently into the perfect law that gives freedom, and continues in it – not forgetting what they have heard, but doing it – they will be blessed in what they do.

James 1:25 NIV

Our words and our mouths create the atmosphere that we're going to have in our homes.

Brenda Timberlake

Wise words satisfy like a good meal; the right words bring satisfaction. The tongue can bring death or life; those who love to talk will reap the consequences.

Proverbs 18:20-21 NLT

As a parent, continually share the Word with your children.

Pat Harrison

❧❧

And you must commit yourselves wholeheartedly to these commands that I am giving you today. Repeat them again and again to your children. Talk about them when you are at home and when you are on the road, when you are going to bed and when you are getting up.

Deuteronomy 6:6-7 NLT

Children learn more by watching what you do than by listening to what you say. They never forget what they observe in the home. Live a life that is worth living—a life lived in Him.

Gloria Copeland

Do not be unequally yoked together with unbelievers. For what fellowship has righteousness with lawlessness? And what communion has light with darkness? ...What part has a believer with an unbeliever? ...For you are the temple of the living God. Therefore "Come out from among them and be separate, says the Lord.

2 Corinthians 6:14-17

If you are not giving the Word to your children, you are not building your house in wisdom and instruction.

Marilyn Hickey

Every wise woman buildeth her house: but the foolish plucketh it down with her hands.

Proverbs 14:1

One of the most refreshing daily exercises that you will ever participate in is the choice to spend time in worship. It is of vital importance that you understand that the time spent in sheer worship is going to enable you to withstand the storms of life.

Carol McLeod

To appoint unto them that mourn in Zion, to give unto them beauty for ashes, the oil of joy for mourning, the garment of praise for the spirit of heaviness; that they might be called trees of righteousness, the planting of the Lord, that he might be glorified.

Isaiah 61:3

Pray God's Word over your husband,
over yourself, and over your children.
Sharon Daugherty

Take the helmet of salvation and the sword of the Spirit, which is the word of God. And pray in the Spirit on all occasions with all kinds of prayers and requests. With this in mind, be alert and always keep on praying for all the Lord's people.

Ephesians 6:17-18 NIV

Fill your house with the Word, and the house will fill up with riches and wealth.

Marilyn Hickey

By wisdom a house is built, and through understanding it is established; through knowledge its rooms are filled with rare and beautiful treasures.

Proverbs 24:3-4 NIV

It is important from the time you are aware of conception to speak the Word to your child.

Pat Harrison

Death and life are in the power of the tongue: and they that love it shall eat the fruit thereof.

Proverbs 18:21

As Christian parents, we must seek God's daily wisdom in every decision that surfaces as a result of simply being a parent!

Margaret Hicks

The young lions do lack, and suffer hunger: but they that seek the Lord shall not want any good thing.

Psalm 34:10

When you are honest with yourself and God, He can create a fresh clean heart and renew a steadfast spirit within you.

Cathy Duplantis

Create in me a pure heart, Oh God, and renew a steadfast spirit within me.

Psalm 51:10 NIV

I believe praise is a powerful weapon against the enemy. Breakthroughts happen as we praise God. He can work a miracle in whatever situation we face regarding our health, finances, family, or career.

Sarah Wehrli

❧

As they began to sing and praise, the Lord set ambushes against the men of Ammon and Moab and Mount Seir who were invading Judah, and they were defeated.

2 Chronicles 20:22

If Jesus had to take time alone with God, then we surely need to.
Sharon Daugherty

One day soon afterward Jesus went up on a mountain to pray, and he prayed to God all night.

Luke 6:19 NLT

Set the right example and walk in love toward your spouse and your children.

Oretha Hagin

That they may teach the young women to be sober, to

love their husbands, to love their children.

Titus 2:4

If you are tender toward God, you'll be tender toward people, including your husband and children.

Sharon Daugherty

❧

This is why I always try to do what I believe is right

before God and people.

Acts 24:16 NCV

Your children need true love and understanding. The only way to give them that love and understanding is to give them God's Word.

Pat Harrsion

We know how much God loves us, and we have put our trust in his love. God is love, and all who live in love live in God, and God lives in them.

I John 4:16 NLT

Nothing will contribute more to a child's well-being and adjustment than growing up in a home where love and appreciation between the parents are evident.

Margaret Hicks

But each one of you must love his wife as he loves himself, and a wife must respect her husband.

Ephesians 5:33 NCV

If you want the assurance that you are participating in God's will for your life on a daily basis, it is vital that you start your day with praise, that you fill it with worship and that you end it with thanksgiving.

Carol McLeod

Bless the Lord, O my soul: and all that is within me, bless his holy name. Bless the Lord, O my soul, and forget not all his benefits

Psalm 103:1-2

One of the best things that parents can do for their children is to develop the right atmosphere in the home, or what I call, "warm the nest."
Marilyn Hickey

And now, dear brothers and sisters, one final thing. Fix your thoughts on what is true, and honorable, and right, and pure, and lovely, and admirable. Think about things that are excellent and worthy of praise. Keep putting into practice all you learned and received from me – everything you heard from me and saw me doing. Then the God of peace will be with you.
Philippians 4:8-9 NLT

There is nothing closer to our hearts than the desire to see children raised in an atmosphere of love, being taught about God and His love.

Margaret Hicks

❧❧

She speaks with wisdom and faithful instruction is

on her tongue.

Proverbs 31:26 NIV

God knows how to deliver your children. Do your part and trust Him to do His.

Gloria Copeland

So you see, the Lord knows how to rescue godly people from their trials, even while keeping the wicked under punishment until the day of final judgment.

2 Peter 2:9 NLT

Our families are in covenant relationship with God, and we overcome the Devil by the blood of the Lamb and by the word of our testimony.

Marilyn Hickey

And they overcame him by the blood of the Lamb, and by the word of their testimony; and they loved not their lives unto the death.

Revelation 12:11

We parents need to pray a wall of protection around our children and grandchildren, commanding Satan to stay away from our children in Jesus' name.

Evelyn Roberts

These miraculous signs will accompany those who believe: They will case out demons in my name,a nd they will speak in new languages.

Mark 16:17 NLT

If you are a believer and you're willing to trust God for the deliverance and salvation of your children, you will not be disappointed.

Gloria Copeland

As the Scripture says, "Anyone who trusts in him will never be disappointed. "

Romans 10:11 NCV

Any sacrifice you might make for your children is not too great a price to pay to be sure your children have the best life possible.

Oretha Hagin

For God so loved the world, that he gave his only begotten Son, that whosoever believeth in him should not perish, but have everlasting life.

John 3:16

If you do not discipline your children, you do not love them.

Pat Harrison

Whoever spares the rod hates their children, but the one who loves their children is careful to discipline them.

Proverbs 13:24 NIV

Discipline begins at home, not in the church or school.

Oretha Hagin

Correct thy son, and he shall give thee rest; yea, he shall give delight unto thy soul.

Proverbs 29:17

Be careful to discipline in love and with a gentle tongue.
Pat Harrison

Wise words satisfy like a good meal; the right

words bring satisfaction.

Proverbs 18:20 NLT

We must be consistent with our children in giving them equal amounts of love and discipline.

Margaret Hicks

Correct your children while there is still hope; do not let them destroy themselves.

Proverbs 19:18 NCV

I

There is a proper way to discipline –
not through anger, but through love.
Pat Harrison

Foolishness is bound in the heart of a child; but the
rod of correction shall drive it far from him.

Proverbs 22:15

I believe it is better to teach children the difference between right and wrong than it is just to teach them a lot of do's and don'ts.

Oretha Hagin

Train children to live the right way, and when they are old, they will not stray from it.

Proverbs 22:6 NCV

Part of your responsibility as a parent is to put up a shield of faith that will help protect your children from the influence of the Evil One.

Gloria Copeland

In addition to all of these, hold up the shield of faith to stop the fiery arrows of the devil.

Ephesians 6:16 NLT

Children need and actually want some boundaries. This creates security in their lives.

Sharon Daugherty

A rod and a reprimand impart wisdom, but a child left undisciplined disgraces its mother.

Proverbs 29:15 NIV

Check up on yourself to make sure you are walking in love and disciplining according to the Word.

Pat Harrison

And walk in love, as Christ also has loved us and given Himself for us, an offering and a sacrifice to Godf or a sweet-smelling aroma.

Ephesians 5:2 NKJV

God understands the life of a mother who is making the effort to seek Him. You can seek Him all through the day. He's listening.

Sharon Daugherty

Hear, O Lord, when I cry with my voice: have mercy also upon me, and answer me. When thou sadist, Seek ye my face; my heart said unto thee, Thy face, Lord, will I seek.

Psalm 27:7-8

By disciplining our children correctly, we not only develop a parent-child relationship, but a friendship as well.
Pat Harrison

Behold, children are a heritage from the Lord. The fruit of the womb is a reward. Happy is the man who has his quiver full of them; they shall not be ashamed, but shall speak with their enemies in the gate.

Psalm 127:3,5 NKJV

Whether you believe it or not, your children will do what you do.

Oretha Hagin

Those things, which ye have both learned, and received, and heard, and seen in me, do: and the God of peace shall be with you.

Philippians 4:9

When children see that they are doing what the Word says, and that the Word works, they will have a desire to do those things.

Pat Harrison

But don't just listen to God's word. You must do what it says. Otherwise, you are only fooling yourselves.

James 1:22 NLT

If you teach your children properly, and show God's love to them when they're young, they won't ever stray very far from the Lord, even when they are older.

Oretha Hagin

❧❧

Fix these words of mine in your hearts and minds; tie them as symbols on your hands and bind them on your foreheads. Teach them to your children, talking about them when you sit at home and when you walk along the road, when you lie down and when you get up.

Deuteronomy 11:18-19 NIV

The way parents talk to their children is vital to their upbringing. Harsh words can eventually cause a child's will to be broken.

Pat Harrison

Some people make cutting remarks, but the words of the wise bring healing.

Proverbs 12:18 NLT

The parent trains through instruction and example.

Sharon Daugherty

Do not irritate and provoke your children to anger [do not exasperate them to resentment], but rear them [tenderly] in the training and discipline and the counsel and admonition of the Lord.

Ephesians 6:4 AMP

We need to have the Word flowing throughout our homes.

Pat Harrison

God's word is alive and working and is sharper than a double-edged sword. It cuts all the way into us, where the soul and the spirit are joined, to the center of our joints and bones. And it judges the thoughts and feelings in our hearts.

Hebrews 4:12 NCV

Your children will respect you and will learn positive habits and attitudes from you when your words and actions are a reflection of your love for God and His Word.

Oretha Hagin

❧

Jesus replied: "Love the Lord your God with all your heart and with all your soul and with all your mind."

Matthew 22:37 NIV

Remember the Word works, and no matter how the circumstances may seem, your child will follow after what he has been taught.

Pat Harrison

We set our eyes not on what we see but on what we cannot see. What we see will last only a short time, but what we cannot see will last forever.

2 Corinthians 4:18 NCV

Be big enough to say to your child,
"I'm sorry."
Pat Harrison

Submitting yourselves one to another in the

fear of God.

Ephesians 5:21

Take up God's strength, shake off
the lies of the enemy, and begin using
what God has put in your hand. As
you offer God what's in your hand, He
will do extraordinary things.

Sarah Wehrli

So we make it our goal to please Him...For Christ's
love compels us because we are convinced that one
died for all,...and those who live should no longer
live for themselves but for him who dies for them
and was raised again.

2 Corinthians 5:9,14-15 NIV

Cultivating discipline in your child will cause him to understand authority and have respect for the people and things around him.

Pat Harrison

Because the Lord disciplines the one he loves, and he chastens everyone he accepts as his son." Endure hardship as discipline; God is treating you as his children. For what children are not disciplined by their father?

Hebrews 12:6-7 NIV

It is so important to provide a happy home for your family. If your children grow up in a good home atmosphere, they will always have pleasant memories of home even as adults.

Oretha Hagin

She watches over the affairs of her household and does not eat the bread of idleness.

Proverbs 31:27 NIV

If the Word can hold the sun and moon in place, then I believe it can answer any need that you and I may have in our families.

Marilyn Hickey

It is the same with my word. I send it out and it always produces fruit. It will accomplish all I want it to, and it will prosper everywhere I send it.

Isaiah 55:11 NLT

When your children come to you for
answers, get your Bible and express
the answer in the simplest way.
Pat Harrison

Your laws are wonderful. No wonder I obey them!

The teaching of your word gives light, so even the

simple can understand.

Psalm 119:129-130 NLT

If you're a believer and willing to trust God for the deliverence and salvation of your children, you'll not be disappointed.

Gloria Copeland

And they of Ephraim shall be like a mighty man, and their heart shall rejoice as through wine: yea, their children shall see it, and be glad; their heart shall rejoice in the Lord. ...I have redeemed them: and they shall increase as they have increased. And I will sow them among the people: and they shall remember me in far countries; and they shall live with their children, and turn again.

Zechariah 10:7-9

See your child through the eyes of God. God has already provided redemptive righteousness for you and your family.

Julie Werner

For he hath made him to be sin for us, who knew no sin; that we might be made the righteousness of God in him.

2 Corinthians 5:21

Each child has a gift within him that will cause him to excel in life. But that gift must be channeled by discipline, love, understanding and knowledge.
Pat Harrison

May our sons flourish in their youth like well-nurtured plants. May our daughters be like graceful pillars, carved to beautify a palace.

Psalm 144:12 NLT

Enjoy your children – God gave
them to you to make you laugh!
Jeanne Caldwell

How joyful is the man whose quiver is full of them!

He will not be put to shame when he confronts his

accusers at the city gates.

Psalm 127:5 NLT

We often fail to realize that redemption has power over the destruction the devil tries to bring on our children's lives.

Gloria Copeland

⁓

Christ hath redeemed us from the curse of the law, being made a curse for us: for it is written, Cursed is every one that hangeth on a tree.

Galatians 3:13

I have found what works for one child is not always effective with the other. Treat each child as a unique individual

Darci Cahill

I praise you because I am fearfully and wonderfully made; your works are wonderful, I know that full well.

Psalm 139:14 NIV

The way a child turns out reflects on the parents. So make sure that you are walking in love.

Pat Harrison

For the entire law if fulfilled in keeping this one command: "Love your neighbor as yourself."

Galatians 5:14 NIV

In order to converse with God, we must learn to speak as God speaks, because we are told that if we ask anything according to His will He hears us.

Germaine Copeland

And this is the confidence that we have in him, that,

if we ask any thing according to his will,

he heareth us.

I John 5:14

Stop looking at your family from your own limited perspective and start seeing it as God sees it – as a power-house.

Gloria Copeland

How should one chase a thousand, and two put ten thousand to flight, except their Rock had sold them, and the Lord had shut them up?

Deuteronomy 32:30

In this day and age, we need the wisdom of God like never before. We cannot only rely on human wisdom or man's intellect; we need supernatural revelation knowledge to live the life that God has call us to live in order to fulfill His purpose.

Sarah Wehrli

He wakens me morning by morning, wakens my ear to listen like one being taught. The Soverign Lord has opened my ears, and I have not been rebellious; I have not drawn back.

Isaiah 50:4-5 NIV

Your children are precious to you. The Scripture calls them a heritage and a reward. You love them so much that you want them to grow and mature into happy, healthy, successful adults.

Gloria Copeland

Their children will be mighty in the land;

the generation of the upright will be blessed.

Psalm 112:2 NIV

Children need strong parental direction and training, the enemy is sure to have free reign in their lives. Taking your place as a godly parent has never been more important.

Gloria Copeland

For I have chosen him, so that he will direct his children and his household after him to keep the way of the Lord by doing what is right and just, so that the Lord will bring about for Abraham what he has promised him.

Genesis 18:19 NIV

Always rely on God's strength and peace in your life. He gives you with peace in troubled times that no one can understand.

Julie Werner

And God's peaace, which is so great we cannot understand it, will keep your hearts and minds in Christ Jesus.

Philippians 4:7 NCV

Guarding your heart is the most ciritcal habit you will ever develop if your desire is to be an emotionally healthy woman.

Carol McLeod

Watch over your heart with all diligence,

for from it flow the springs of life.

Proverbs 4:23 NASB

It is important to train your children to walk with God on a daily basis by reading the Word, praying, and spending time with Him. Teach them to desire spiritual things and help them learn to "walk in the Spirit."

Gloria Copeland

But I say, walk and live [habitually] in the [Holy] Spirit [responsive to and controlled and guided by the Spirit]; then you will certainly not gratify the cravings and desires of the flesh (of human nature without God).

Galatians 5:16 AMP

God is always faithful to fulfill what He has promised. He promises to strengthen and help you.

Julie Werner

Don't be afraid, for I am with you.

Don't be discouraged, for I am your God.

I will strengthen you and help you.

I will hold you up with my victorious right hand.

Isaiah 41:10 NLT

If the desire of your heart is to come after Christ and to pursue Him only, it takes one significant choice. Press into Christ Jesus and follow Him wholeheartedly.

Carol McLeod

Then Jesus said to His disciples, "If anyone wishes to come after Me, he must deny himself, and take up his cross and follow Me."

Matthew 16:24 NASB

Most of all, be mindful that living a godly life before your children is the best teacher! Provide a solid home with love and support, and show them by example how to live seperated unto God.

Gloria Copeland

Flee also youthful lusts; but pursue righteousness, faith, love, peace with those who call on the Lord out of a pure heart.

2 Timothy 2:22 NKJV

Replace your weariness with God's perfect peace for your life. The spiritual opposite for weariness is the simplicity of abiding in Christ.

Carol McLeod

Abide in Me, and I in you. As the branch cannot bear fruit of itself, unless it abides in the vine, neither can you, unless you abide in Me.

John 15:4 NKJV

Each person receives love differently.
Find out your child's Love Language.
My son David is physical touch. My
daughter, Maryclaire like quality time.
Darci Cahill

Love suffers long and is kind; love does not envy;
love does not parade itself, is not puffed up; does
not behave rudely, does not seek its own, is not pro-
voked, thinks no evil; does not rejoice in iniquity,
but rejoices in the truth; bears all things, believes all
things, hopes all things, endures all things.

Love never fails...

1 Corinthians 13:4-8 NKJV

PRAYER OF SALVATION

God loves you—no matter who you are, no matter what your past. God loves you so much that He gave His one and only begotten Son for you. The Bible tells us that "...whoever believes in Him shall not perish but have eternal life" (John 3:16 NIV). Jesus laid down His life and rose again so that we could spend eternity with Him in heaven and experience His absolute best on earth. If you would like to receive Jesus into your life, say the following prayer out loud and mean it from your heart.

Heavenly Father, I come to You admitting that I am a sinner. Right now, I choose to turn away from sin, and I ask You to cleanse me of all unrighteousness. I believe that Your Son, Jesus, died on the cross to take away my sins. I also believe that He rose again from the dead so that I might be forgiven of my sins and made righteous through faith in Him. I call upon the name of Jesus Christ to be the Savior and Lord of my life. Jesus, I choose to follow You and ask that You fill me with the power of the Holy Spirit. I declare that right now I am a child of God. I am free from sin and full of the righteousness of God. I am saved in Jesus' name. Amen.

If you prayed this prayer to receive Jesus Christ as your Savior for the first time, please contact us on the Web at **www.harrisonhouse.com** to receive a free book.

Or you may write to us at

Harrison House • P.O. Box 35035 • Tulsa, Oklahoma 74153